The Stars That Smile

By
Jodi O'Donnell-Ames

Interior illustrations by
Alina N. O'Donnell

Open Door Kids by

Open Door Publications, LLC

Acknowledgements

Thanks go to Mike Budden, a gifted artist, for a beautiful cover illustration, and to the many people who have read and encouraged me to write this story. Also, a special thank you to the Hope Loves Company Board. Your dedication to HLC means the world to me.

Table of Contents

Chapter One 8
Chapter Two 14
Chapter Three 20
Chapter Four 24
Chapter Five 28
Chapter Six 32
About Amyotrophic Lateral Sclerosis 35
Especially for Parents 39
ALS Resources 44
About Hope Loves Company 47
About the Author 49
About the Illustrator 50

Chapter One

Sarah sat next to her mommy at the breakfast table. Mommy was having hot buttered toast and honey. Like every morning, Sarah was starving and couldn't inhale breakfast quickly enough to silence the growls of her unruly stomach. Sarah's mom had plopped her head alongside the plate of toast, resting her forehead on her folded arms. Her hair was messy. Sarah touched her mommy's knotted hair and her mommy, scooping her arm under the table, held Sarah's other hand. When

Sarah was mid-bite of her usual breakfast of crunchy oats, raisins and bananas, her mommy lifted her head, rubbed her eyes and began to speak.

"Have you thought about riding your bike in the Fourth of July parade tomorrow?" Then her eyes fluttered, begging to close.

Sarah stopped chewing. She placed her spoon on the table and slid the bowl away.

It was only last summer when Sarah and her daddy had decorated their bikes with streamers and flags and joined the excited marchers in the parade. But this year was different.

"Do I have to be in the parade tomorrow?" Sarah wanted to know.

Sarah's mom lifted her coffee mug to take a sip and had a bite of toast. Then she wiped her mouth free of sticky crumbs, put her hand on Sarah's arm and said, "But you made a special hat and shirt for the parade, aren't you excited?"

The truth was that things were different this year and Sarah was anything but excited. She wanted to forget what made this year different. She wanted to forget that her daddy could no longer walk and needed a wheelchair. Yesterday, there was a beeping noise, and then a truck pulled into her driveway and left a wheelchair, Daddy's wheelchair. Sarah wanted to scream how mad she felt because her daddy's disease, which was called Lou Gehrig's Disease, made his muscles soft and weak. She wanted to yell, WHY MY DADDY? But instead she muttered, "No."

"But I thought that you loved parades," Mommy said.

"Not anymore," said Sarah. "May I be excused? I'm not hungry."

Sarah's mom nodded yes.

It was exactly one year ago that Sarah knew something was wrong. She and Daddy were playing soccer when Daddy fell. He fell several times, and he was normally very good at soccer. When Daddy took a shot at the goal, he fell hard and needed help standing again.

After that, Sarah had many visits with Grammy and Poppy while Mommy and Daddy went to see different doctors.

At first, the doctors and her parents weren't too worried. But when no one could figure out what was wrong with Daddy's wobbly legs, everyone was worried.

It was soon before the Fourth of July parade last year that Daddy was told he had Lou Gehrig's Disease.

Now, a year later, Sarah hoped to make the disease disappear. On her way to Daddy's room, she saw her magic wand from her fairy princess costume, shimmering on the carpet. Delighted, she gave it a

whirl and said, "Abracadabra!"
After she hopped onto Daddy's
messy bed, among blankets and
pillows, and showered his cheeks
with kisses, she asked, "Can you
walk now, Sleepyhead?"

Daddy smiled. His face was
scratchy. He tried to move his
hand closer to Sarah but his hand
wouldn't budge.

"Why don't you come snuggle
with me, Sarah?"

Sarah snuggled next to her
daddy's warmth and waited for his
answer.

"No, sweetie, I still can't walk,
but that won't keep me from
parading with my princess! We
have lots of decorating to do today
if we want to look patriotic
tomorrow."

Sarah hopped off the bed and
dropped her magic wand into the
trash can where it hit the bottom
with a clang.

"That's no magic wand!" she
muttered as she left the room.

Chapter Two

Mommy was in the hallway, leaning against the wall, her eyes shut. She had heard everything.

Sarah didn't care.

"I don't want to be in the parade tomorrow if the wheelchair has to be in the parade, too! Send it back."

Mommy started to speak, "But he needs..." and then, she stopped. She watched as Sarah disappeared down the hallway and into her playroom.

There, among games and Legos and Barbie clothes, Sarah

sat in front of her dollhouse. She found the mom, dad and child dolls and placed them in the dollhouse kitchen. In her dollhouse, the daddy could walk, and Sarah made him walk around the tiny kitchen. The daddy could play soccer. And the daddy did not need a wheelchair or help getting in and out of bed. Playing with her dolls was usually fun, but today it wasn't, so Sarah put the dolls down, and started decorating the dollhouse front porch for the dolls' pretend Fourth of July parade.

While Sarah played with her dollhouse, she tried not to think about the wheelchair and her daddy's disease. She decorated her dollhouse just the way she liked it, without a wheelchair in sight.

Meanwhile, Mommy turned and headed back into the bedroom to get Daddy up and ready for the day. He needed help getting out of bed and into his wheelchair. He needed help getting his teeth brushed and his hair combed, and he needed help getting dressed and eating meals.

A little while later the whirring and knocking hum of the wheelchair told Sarah that Daddy was on his way to the playroom and, of course, Mommy wasn't far behind.

The dollhouse family was enjoying bacon and eggs when Daddy clumsily maneuvered his way into the playroom.

"Your dollhouse is ready for the parade!" said Daddy, entering the playroom. "I'm ready for pancakes, then decorating."

"The flag looks festive on the front porch," added Mommy.

Sarah stood to get a better view of Daddy. She pointed at the wheelchair. "That should be in a hospital for really sick people," she said.

Sarah watched as her daddy tried to steer his wheelchair where he wanted to go, next to her.

"Watch out!" screamed Sarah.

But it was too late. The chair lurched forward and scraped the wall, and then it jerked backwards with a crunch, right into the dollhouse. Flecks of paint and wood peppered the carpet.

"I'm so sorry, sweetie. I'm not the best driver yet. I'll fix your dollhouse as soon as Uncle Joe can help me."

Daddy had made the dollhouse as a surprise for Sarah's very first birthday. When she turned four, she began decorating it, room by room. It was her very favorite toy.

Sarah felt hot, as if something was boiling inside of her. It boiled and bubbled until she couldn't keep it inside any longer.

"None of the other daddies I know have wheelchairs! None of the other daddies I know can't feed themselves. Why can't you get better?"

Sarah turned and ran out of the playroom, down the hallway

and into her bedroom. Mommy followed close behind.

Chapter Three

When Mommy entered the room, Sarah was lying in bed hugging her pillow. Her face was red, and she whispered, "I wish Daddy could still walk and didn't need a wheelchair."

Mommy snuggled close and whispered back, "Me, too."

Mommy grabbed two tissues from Sarah's bureau. The two lay there quietly until Sarah spoke.

"Why is Daddy sick?"

"No one knows why Daddy is sick," explained Mommy. "The doctors don't know what causes

Lou Gehrig's Disease or how to cure it. They are working on it though. And while Daddy can no longer walk, or run, or even build the things he wants to build, he is still the same Daddy who loves his princess more than anything! Your Daddy is so brave, and he is doing the best he can."

Sarah closed her sore eyes, and then opened them again. She looked around her room. She saw a picture of herself with Daddy, standing next to their bikes at last year's parade. She saw the flute, which Daddy had whittled for Sarah when she turned three. She saw the beautifully painted butterflies that hung from her ceiling—a gift from Daddy last spring.

Daddy peered from the hallway into Sarah's room.

His face was red, too.

"Are my princesses okay?" he asked.

Mommy and Sarah nodded their heads yes.

"I'm ready for my first breakfast. Sarah, are you ready for your second?"

Mommy sat up, wiped her face and said, "I know I am!"

The second breakfast was way better than the first. Daddy requested pancakes topped with strawberries, honey and whipped cream.

After breakfast Mommy took Daddy to physical therapy while Amy, the sitter, stayed with Sarah. Amy loved playing soccer, so she played goalie while Sarah took shots. Lots of shots. By the time her parents returned, Sarah was exhausted.

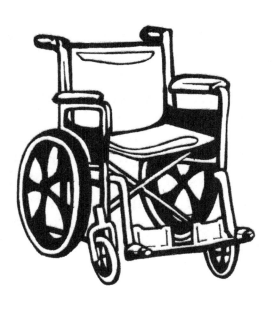

Chapter Four

After dinner, with a full belly, Sarah fell asleep on the couch, dirty cleats and all.

But before her dreams took hold, she heard Daddy's voice, "We need to get that dollhouse fixed right away."

Then Mommy's voice, too, "I'll call Joe in the morning."

Daddy continued before Sarah faded...

"I need to learn how to work this wheelchair better. Please help me outside before it gets dark so I can practice zooming around the yard until I'm ready for NASCAR!"

Later that night, someone was tapping Sarah's back.

"Time for your bath, Princess," said Mommy.

Sarah was so dirty that her bubbles turned gray when Mommy came in to wash her back. She kissed Sarah's head and ran warm water while adding more bubbles. Then she gently washed Sarah's back and hair and rinsed the frothy soap off before helping to dry off with a great, big towel.

"You don't have to be in the parade tomorrow," said Mommy, "if you don't want to."

"Probably not," replied Sarah, stepping into her pajamas. "Whose turn is it to read tonight?"

Mommy thought about it for a moment. "It's Daddy's night," she said. He ordered you a new book; he'll start it tonight but you know what he'll say before kissing you goodnight."

Sarah laughed, "Yup, since I was a teeny tiny newborn who weighed less than a Chihuahua!"

The bed felt extra cozy. Daddy read for ten minutes until Sarah felt her eyes rest, just for a minute. She knew what was coming next.

"Good night stars. Good night air. Good night noises everywhere," said Daddy as he turned his wheelchair and rolled out of the room.

Chapter Five

In the middle of the night, when her parents were sound asleep, Sarah awoke. The house was quiet, but Sarah's head wasn't. She grabbed her favorite photo album from her bookshelf. She looked at all of the pictures her mom and dad had taken of her since she was a baby.

She looked at the photograph of Daddy holding both of her hands and helping her to walk when she was just one year old.

Daddy taught me how to walk. I wasn't always so good at

it. I used to fall and stumble without help, just like he does now, she thought to herself.

She looked at another photo, taken two summers before while they vacationed at the beach.

Daddy taught me how to body surf. We rode the ocean's waves again and again. We were two happy fish until our hands were prunes and our eyes salty sore.

She turned the page.

Daddy took me camping in our yard. His muscles were too weak to put up the tent without Uncle Joe's help. But even though he felt sick, Daddy, Mommy and I had a campfire and s'mores and told ghost stories. He showed me the Big Dipper and my first shooting star.

Suddenly, Sarah had an idea. She tiptoed into the playroom and got paper, scissors, markers and glitter. She taped up the tattered Uncle Sam's hat that she had made at school. Then she rummaged through her drawers until she found the right clothes. Tired but happy, Sarah fell back into bed.

Chapter Six

"Wake up, Sleepyheads!" Sarah giggled the next morning, knocking on her parents' bedroom door. With a running start, she jumped into bed right between her parents.

"Daddy, let's be in the parade today. I can sit on your lap, and we can drive the wheelchair together."

Daddy grinned, "Nothing would make me happier, Sarah!"

"Great!" Sarah grabbed Mommy's hand and dashed her out of the room. They returned moments later with the decorated wheelchair.

"Surprise!"

The wheelchair was covered in sparkling red, white and blue stars.

"Did you do this all by yourself?"

"Yup."

"But when?"

"Very early. When you and the sun were still sleepyheads."

Mommy helped Daddy out of bed and into the wheelchair. Sarah placed the Uncle Sam hat on his head, slanted and silly, just the way she liked it.

"Makes me look handsome!" said Daddy.

By the time Daddy and Sarah joined the marchers, the parade was in full swing.

"Hot dogs here! Get your nice juicy hot dogs here!" shouted a man pushing a cart. Mommy waved and cheered from the sidewalk. Sarah sat high on Daddy's lap.

"Want to steer, Sarah?" Daddy asked. Sarah smiled, then made the wheelchair go forward, clumsily. "I'll practice zooming around the yard until I'm ready for NASCAR," she said.

They zigzagged along the street. A clown squirted Sarah with a water gun. The water felt cool on hot, sticky skin.

"Are you having a good time, Princess?" Daddy asked.

"No. I'm having a GREAT time. You're fun!" Sarah said.

A smile grew on Daddy's face, a familiar smile. It was as big as the ocean and as bright as a shooting star. Just like Sarah's. Just the way she liked it.

About
Amyotrophic Lateral Sclerosis

By Terry Heiman-Patterson, MD

Amyotrophic Lateral Sclerosis (ALS), often referred to as Lou Gehrig's Disease, is the most common degenerative disease of the adult motor system. It causes damage to motor neurons as they travel from the brain to the spinal cord as well as the motor neurons that travel from the base of the brain and the spinal cord to the muscles. This loss of motor neurons is responsible for progressive weakness.

ALS generally begins between 55 and 75 years of age, although all ages can be involved. It can affect men slightly than women, with a ratio of approximately 1.5 to 1.

There are about 20-30 new cases for every million people, while at any one time there are about 20 people living with ALS for every million people. This means that across the United States there are about 30,000 people with ALS, and there are people living with ALS all around the world.

People with ALS develop progressive weakness that can begin with speech or swallowing difficulties, or loss of strength in either an arm or leg. Along with the weakness, there can be wasting of the muscles and twitching. Wherever it begins, the disease rapidly spreads from one area to the next, leading to weakness in all of the limbs, inability to speak or swallow and difficulties with breathing, with little time to adjust to each new loss. The person living with ALS becomes totally dependent on others for everything. The entire family is affected both physically and emotionally by the inexorable progression and almost daily changes in function.

The cause of ALS remains unknown, and given the variation in presentation and the multiple genes now identified, it is likely that ALS is a complex disorder. While we have no cures, there is treatment. One drug, Riluzole, has been identified that slows the disease modestly. In addition, there is optimized clinical care through multidisciplinary clinics that address the physical and emotional needs of people who are living with ALS, as well as providing support to families and caregivers. These centers provide hope through the best available care, improved quality of life and clinical research.

Dr. Terry Heiman-Patterson is Professor and Vice Chairman of the Department of Neurology as well as the Chief of Neuromuscular diseases at Drexel University College of Medicine. She directs the MDA/ALS Center of

Hope at Drexel and also the MDA Clinic at Good Shepherd Rehabilitation Hospital in Allentown, Pennsylvania.

She trained in neuromuscular diseases at the University of Pennsylvania.

Especially for Parents

By Jodi O'Donnell-Ames

I am a certified teacher and have worked with children for most of my life. I have also raised three children who have lost a parent to ALS and understand how complicated life becomes for everyone in the family when a parent is ill. With that in mind, I have included a few suggestions below, which were helpful to me and may be helpful to you.

It Takes a Village. People living with ALS need support. Caregivers need support, and so will other family members, especially children. Be sure to let school teachers and counselors know what your family is facing. Patients and caregivers will have less time to be parents. Be sure to ask trusted family and friends who have children of a similar age to include your child on fun excursions. Allow your child to be a child.

Other Helpers. A trusted relative or friend who does not have children can also be helpful. He or she can provide special bonding time such as a day at the beach or amusement park, and the one-on-one time may provide an opportunity for your child to share feelings about the situation. Encourage the adult to listen to the child, but not to necessarily bring up the family situation on each and every outing. Sometimes your child may just need time to do ordinary things without thinking about what is going on at home.

Special Reading Time. Try to find uninterrupted, quiet time to read this book with your child or have him or her read it to you. Be patient and allow enough time for questions, and answer those questions to the best of your ability. Listen closely and you will learn what he or she already knows. Remember that young children often want to hear the same information, or the same story read to them, more than once. Be patient and allow them to choose this or other books that relate to their parent's illness as often as they would like. As they grow and learn they may have new questions, or need more complex answers to the same questions.

When You Can't Be There. When one parent is ill, the other parent must divide his or her time. When you can't be there in person, find creative ways to remember your child. Leave notes in hiding spots, or buy and wrap a small surprise to place under the pillow. Make a video of family memories that your child can view while you are at the hospital.

Involve Your child. If a child expresses an interest in caregiving, allow it. Helping is a form of affection and may provide feelings of pride and accomplishment. The reverse is also true. A child may be uninterested in caregiving. Don't make your child responsible for taking care of a parent in ways he or she is not yet ready for. Allow the parent to be a parent and the child to be a child as much as possible.

Pay Attention. Kids cope and grieve differently. Some children may become withdrawn, while others may get angry. Think before you react to your child's behavior. Was there another change in the PAL's (Person with ALS) condition? Did Mom just get a feeding tube? Did another PAL acquaintance lose his battle and your child overhear the news?

Love Your Child. Showering your child with love, whether you are the parent with ALS or the caregiving parent, is the most important thing of all. Forming great memories of love and affecttion are healing for the entire family. Document those memories on camera and video. If you have the energy and strength, write love letters to your child for special occasions down the road. These will certainly be cherished.

ALS Resources

Organizations for People Living With ALS & Their Caregivers

Hope Loves Company
www.hopelovescompany.com

The ALS Hope Foundation
www.alshopefoundation.org

The ALS Association
www.alsa.org

Les Turner ALS Foundation
www.lesturnerals.org

Team Gleason
www.teamgleason.org

The MDA
http://mda.org/disease/amyotrophic-lateral-sclerosis

The Kevin Turner Foundation
www.kevinturnerfoundation.org

TEAM Cure ALS Foundation
http://www.scoop.it/t/alsawareness

ALS Connections

http://als.myupsite.com/

Support and Forums

TEAM Cure ALS Foundation
http://www.scoop.it/t/alsawareness

ALS Connections
http://als.myupsite.com/

Share the Care
http://www.sharethecare.org/

ALS forums
www.alsforums.com/

ALSTDI
http://www.als.net/

For Children

What Did You Learn Today?
by Tina Singer Ames
http://www.amazon.com/What-did-you-learn-today/dp/B0006RNTG4

Grandpa, What is ALS?
by Bonnie Gold-Babins

Hope Loves Company
www.hopelovescompany.com

http://kidshealth.org/kid/grownup/conditions/als.html#

Facebook page for the children, grandchildren and young adults of people living with ALS
https://www.facebook.com/groups/hlckidsconnect/

About
Hope Loves Company

Hope Loves Company is a non-profit organization dedicated to providing both emotional and educational support to children and young adults who have parents or family members living with ALS.

The organization is the result of raising three children who have learned about ALS (or Lou Gehrig's Disease) as young children. Kevin Gerard O'Donnell, late husband of Jodi O'Donnell, heroically battled ALS from 1995 until his passing in 2001. Their daughter, Alina, was almost three when Kevin was diagnosed. She did not understand why her daddy was different from the other daddies and asked many questions over the years.

In 2003, Jodi O'Donnell married Warren Ames and became the mother of his two children, Nora and Adam, who were then age ten and seven. Nora and Adam lost their biological mother, Tina Singer Ames, to ALS in 2000.

ALS has united the O'Donnell and Ames families in hope and love. Not a day goes by without remembering Kevin and Tina and the lessons they have shared. Hope Loves Company was formed in their memories.

For more information go to:
www.hopelovescompany.com,
or email:
hopelovescompany@gmail.com

You can find out more about Hope Loves Company and its mission by watching a video at:
http://www.youtube.com/watch?v=p2pzXRbx_vs

About the Author

Jodi O'Donnell-Ames is a certified teacher, writer, massage therapist, member of Union Fire Co. and Rescue Squad and tireless advocate for people with Lou Gehrig's Disease, or ALS (Amyotrophic Lateral Sclerosis). She is also the founder and president of Hope Loves Company, a non-profit organization committed to helping the children and grandchildren of people living with ALS. She lives with her husband, Benton, and three wonderful children in New Jersey.

About the Illustrator

Alina O'Donnell is currently studying English and Environmental Studies at the University of Delaware. She has been involved with Hope Loves Company since its inception and has always loved to doodle and paint since her first art class at age two.

CPSIA information can be obtained
at www.ICGtesting.com
Printed in the USA
BVOW08s1459110418
513049BV00005B/10/P